WHEN THERE ARE NO SECRETS

Books by C.G. Hanzlicek

Poetry:

Living In It
Stars
Calling the Dead
When There Are No Secrets

Translations:

A Bird's Companion
Mirroring: Selected Poems of Vladimir Holan

C.G. Hanzlicek

WHEN THERE ARE NO SECRETS

Carnegie-Mellon University Press
Pittsburgh 1986

ACKNOWLEDGMENTS

Some of these poems have appeared in *Cimarron Review, The North American Review, Poetry Now,* and *Three Rivers Poetry Journal.*

The sequence of poems, "A Dozen for Leah, My Daughter, Born April 29, 1980," was originally published as a chapbook from Brandenburg Press.

The publication of this book is supported by grants from the National Endowment for the Arts in Washington, D.C., a Federal agency, and from the Pennsylvania Council on the Arts.

Carnegie-Mellon University Press books are distributed by Harper and Row.

Library of Congress Catalog Card Number 85-71691
ISBN 0-88748-056-X
ISBN 0-88748-057-8 pbk.
Copyright © 1986 by C.G. Hanzlicek
All rights reserved
Printed and bound in the United States of America
First Edition

CONTENTS

1

When There Are No Secrets............... 10
The Accidents........................... 11
Inward 12
Bays.................................... 13
Evening Light 14
The Bell is Struck....................... 15
In the Mountains........................ 16
Night................................... 17
Northern Pike........................... 18
Owl..................................... 19
Slough 20
Flycasting at Sunset..................... 21
My Instinct and My Answer 22
Jay..................................... 23
Toward Sleep 24
I Don't Blame You....................... 25
In the Dark Again 26
A Short Ode to My Shoes.................. 27
C.G. Hanzlicek.......................... 28
Waves................................... 29

2

A Dozen for Leah 32

3

Summer Night 48
Bill's Well.............................. 49
Fresno July 50
Letters................................. 52
On a Highway South of Minneapolis........ 53
One Humble Citizen...................... 54

4

Insomnia 56
Landlocked 57
Evening Rain. 58
Body and Soul 59
Dear Ophelia. 60
Journey. 61
Simple Truths. 62

5

The Long Arc 66

For Bruce & Marsha Boston

1

When There Are No Secrets

Yesterday the bed
Was turned and raked smooth,
Today you come to it
With the trowel
And a little mesh bag of anemone bulbs.
The soil, still damp,
Is sweet as you bend to it.
You poke a hole with the trowel handle
And drop in a dry bulb.
Your eye is caught by a robin,
His head cocked to hear
Worms feeling their way in the dark.
As he hops a foot further,
You see something else...
There are footprints
Beneath your bedroom window.
They are sunk deep in the earth.
Someone stood still there
For hours, listening
To you feel your way in the dark.

The Accidents

Late night,
And the air suddenly
Sits down on the sky's sofa
For a rest.
A flash of lightning,
And the row of elms
Takes a giant step closer.
Steps, flashes,
So many accidents to shape a life...
Some so powerful they
Could split
An elm from crown to root,
And others long low rumbles
That rattle grandmother's teacups.
Between the two to say:
If not for you, I'd have been someone else.
To bow to the accidents and say:
I'm content with you,
And sometimes,
Sometimes even with me.

Inward

We look inward
And at first it is empty
As a museum between exhibitions.
Then we see a child
Staring at a blank wall, mute,
Who stopped asking
When no one bothered to answer.
In another room, an old man
Shuffles worn cards
For solitaire,
The only game in town.
A woman weeps
Into her hands,
A canary is dying of neglect,
Memories gather
In the corners like dust.
This is why our houses
Have so many windows.

Bays

Bays are odd.
People on the points
Live sometimes for weeks in fog.
They paint kitchens gray.
They wear
Old sweatshirts like uniforms.
They develop a bitter language
With one adjective.
They forget an egg
Can be cooked sunny side up.
They forget
That if you hold the door open
The fly will leave of its own accord.
They resent the band of light
On the inland shore.
Finally there's the day
That totally breaks them,
And they begin
To hate the nearby sun
For being a crowd pleaser.

Evening Light

I prefer the light of evening.
Mornings, the shadows head west.
They have the confidence of pioneers,
But they are cooled by dew
And are too full of themselves.

By late afternoon, shadows
Have learned what it is to be human.
They make a gesture and stretch
Toward where the sun will rise,
But really they just want to sleep.

The Bell is Struck

Night,
I'm so content with you,
It must be I have something to hide.
Three crickets
Are working harder than I ever did.
A fourth joins
With a totally new idea,
And the ash leaves let out their sigh.
I listen.
Given what I am,
I've been just about
As good as I can be.
The moon is heavy
As a temple bell where it is day now.
I really listen.
The bell is struck only one time,
But the sound seems to gather for hours.
Where it is day now,
People find a way to pray.
I listen to the moon.

In the Mountains

The mirror hangs by a rope
From a low limb.
To shave means daily scrutiny

Of the corners of the mouth,
The slope under the chin
Where time passes

And leaves its tracks.
Over nine thousand mornings
I've lathered my face;

You'd think I'd know
All about it by now.
Nine thousand inspections,

But when a wind from nowhere
Slowly turns the mirror,
It's a shock to see

What's there when my face is gone:
A plane of gray, flat gray,
Reflecting nothing.

Night

My fingertips scrape straw
As I probe the underbody
Of a fat black hen.
I get pecked hard on the forearm,
But I pull out
A still warm egg.
Hours later, I crack it
On the lip of a dark blue bowl,
And the sun comes out.
I eat, wait for night.

Northern Pike

Like a submerged log
Flecked by silvery bark
He patrols where the river is deepest.
Four treble-hooked lures
Hang from his lip,
Flags from the old wars.
He'll die a natural death;
He's too heavy
And full of turns to be caught now.
He's the river itself
Turned into an animal,
His belly
Full of the young.

Owl

Who is forbidden?
He's known all his life long.
My claws contract
Until they break the branch;
As sure as I'm a god,
He knows,
Yet he must ask:
Who? Who?

Who is permitted?
Who loves just one thing
That breathes,
Even himself if it comes to that,
Can walk beneath my oak.
My talons
Will only be question marks
Wrapped around a limb.

Slough

An egret sleeps on one leg
Like a white flag in the shallows,
But it's the frogs
Who will singly and surely surrender
To the egret
All that they have
In one last green croak.

Wading the reedbed for bass,
I speak my first words of this dawn,
And my voice cracks and croaks.
I know I share my fate with the frog
Carrying my hook on his back,
But at the top of the food chain,
It almost sounds like I'm singing.

Flycasting at Sunset

Ripe wheat runs down the hillside
To where the lily pads begin.
I launch the canoe
And paddle through waveless water
The color of whiskey.
Purple martins
Clear the insects from my course.
I have no anchor;
I ship the oar and drift.
With a pliers
I straighten and bend the hook
On my fly until it snaps,
Then cast out as far as I can
And wait for stars.

My Instinct and My Answer

A harbor seal and a sea lion
Washed up dead this morning.
Something has nibbled at
The harbor seal's face;
It wears a blank mask of white flesh.

I steer my daughter clear,
She doesn't see them,
But my wife is full of questions:
Shouldn't we report them?
Were they shot?

Won't someone want to look them over
To see how they died?
My instinct and my answer
Is to let them be,
Let the tide take their heaviness back,

Let whatever tasted the harbor seal
Have done with it down to bone.
She isn't at all satisfied.
To tell the truth, neither am I.
Perhaps the sea is.

Jay

One soaring squawk from him
And doves pecking millet under the feeder
Fold their tents
And clatter for cover.

I won't deny his meanness.

Both robins and towhees
Lost their spring eggs to jays
In our neighbor's yard.
Now he's armed with a pellet gun
And threatens
To shoot looters on sight.

Yet there's something about a jay...

The way he hones his heavy beak
On the rim of the birdbath,
And that dark craft in his eye.
He's figured out how to jam
Pecans between fence boards
To crack his way to the meat.

Even the one-legged one
Has made his loud visits
For three years now.

If the last insect on earth
Is a cockroach,
The last bird will be a jay,
And the jay will
Stake out his claim with a shriek,
Take three bouncing steps,
And eat the roach.

Toward Sleep

Like a freight train
Hauling a hundred cars up a long grade
In the middle of the Mojave,
I climb toward sleep.

It's been a good day.
A man who all his life was up to no good
Died; everyone I loved yesterday
Is still alive today.

My daughter asked me
To be a bear, and for ten minutes
I lumbered on all fours through her world,
Making her laugh at the terror of joy.

Stars suddenly fill the dark roof
Of my skull, like sparks
Rising when the last big log
Is thrown on the campfire at midnight.

I Don't Blame You

You listened,
And you heard a woman
In the next apartment crying
Over one potato
To be divided five ways.

When you looked,
On your sidewalk two little girls
Twirled a rope
While another jumped,
Absent-mindedly touching
A blue swollen place on her cheek.

Whatever you put in your mouth
Tasted like your mother's
Ashes.
Everything smelled like rust.

I don't blame you for locking,
One by one,
All five of your doors.
The senses shouldn't be open
Wounds that throb like a bad tooth
When air passes over them.

The worst arrived
When you pulled all the shades
And lay down in the dark,
Betrayed
Even by your eyelids.

In the Dark Again

Like a stone dropping down a well
The moon sets,
And once again I'm in the dark.
Oh, there's Vega and Rigel,
But the trees are black,
The crickets lost in the grass.
I've come this far
On two blind wings and no prayer,
But it feels natural,
It works,
And I'm not where I once was.
Forward is something,
Even if there are no high beams
To make the mile markers
Blaze along the road.
Besides, if it all had a single
Readable meaning,
Flashing like a blue beer sign,
I'd keep brushing it
Like a moth,
Lightly,
Without a thought in my head.

A Short Ode to My Shoes
(Red Wing 565 58313T7 10½ B)

Their hides begin to glow at dawn,
Twelve eyes
And twelve hooks of brass
Wait to be snugged to the tongues.
They are molds cast by my walk;
As I pull them on,
Wrinkles mark where my toes bend,
And there are softened pockets
For my ankle bones.
Guilt is never thrown away on me,
I'll admit to anything,
But I will not apologize to this cow
Whose flesh I wear so well.
Put stones in my path,
And I'll tread them like cobbles.
I have Red Wings,
I can be resoled,
So point me to the road;
Now I am shod.

C.G. Hanzlicek
(after Atilla Jozsef)

Take my word for it, Hanzlicek,
I love you,
I can't help myself.
I live with a woman
Who wakes to your needs
And doesn't hate me for them.

We can compare life
To a worn shoe,
A car out of gas on a back road,
A lost ticket,
Yet in the end, beyond the metaphors,
We can't help loving life.

It would be nice
To buy a ticket to the self;
It must be somewhere inside.
We might arrive, thought,
Too bored from the journey
To want to see the sights.

We might just lie on our back
In the hotel room,
Counting brass spindles
On the footrail of the bed,
Having our meals sent up,
Dreaming another self.

Waves

The oldest dwellers
On this stretch of coast
Thought the sky
Rocked gently up and down.
Each time the sky rim
Touched the sea,
It pushed out a wave.
What does make waves?
It's windless,
It must have to do with gravity,
But as the last sliver
Of the sun rocks on the horizon,
The old science will do.
For days now,
At the exact moment the sun
Slips into the sea,
In a silence broken only by waves,
I've had the feeling
I know what I want.
It's ridiculous,
It's so simple
It must not be it.
On the other hand...

2

A Dozen for Leah, My Daughter, Born April 29, 1980

1.
Four times in the final four hours
The doctor's gloved, greased hand
Forced to the top of your head.
The push backward,
Against the ridges of muscle,
Against the first law,
Was meant to make you rotate,
But you would not turn;
Looking upward was your first desire.

When they said it was time to wait no more,
They pulled you into time.
While they sewed the firey slash
Across your mother's belly,
A nurse ran you down the hall to me.
Under the warmer,
Against my naked chest,
Our skins were soon bonded
In a slippery film of sweat.
I inhaled again the cheesy sweetness
That had flowed onto your mother's thighs
Each time she'd arched her back and pushed.
I read the river map
Of your blood, the blood of three,
Printed on your skull,
And when I cupped
The whole of your head in my hand,
You looked up —
True to what I already knew of you —
Up into my eyes.
You looked at me so long, with such calm,

I began to feel almost innocent.
It must feel like that.

Later, whenever I carried you
Outside for a look at the world,
You never looked down at roses,
Columbine, daffodils,
But always up into the sway of trees,
Your head swaying with them,
Or even higher,
Tracking the soar of swallows,
Your mouth open in awe,
Your eyes at home.

2.

Why this difference?
Around others, a holding back,
A defense layered by shyness,
But around you,
I'm transformed into a Cosmic Bozo;
I'll do anything for a laugh:
Diaper my head,
Pack my cheeks with big wooden beads,
Hang your socks from my ears,
And in my floppy sheepskin slippers
Do the dance of the manic duck.
I'm your circus,
Your laughter is my calliope.

3.

A cricket and stars shape the night.
Orion has a good bit of the sky
All to himself.

It will be many years
Before you begin to understand
How far away he is,

How remote
Everything in the night sky is from us.
There is nothing so cold

As the space between stars.
Nothing, that is,
But the distances between people.

The cricket is close,
So close I can feel my eardrums vibrate.
You like his lullaby.

You hum along with him awhile,
Then your knees go limp at my sides,
And your head rolls to rest on my shoulder.

You softly snore in my ear,
And the shape of my life grows larger;
Orion seems to move closer.

4.

Your first word was not mama or papa.
We are constants, named or not;
One of us is there always,
Slow as the moon,
In the center of your eye.
You wanted to name
The elusive being,
The one that caught the corner of your eye
And darted through your vision so fast
It was truly miraculous.
So you listened hard,
And then you spoke it:
Bird... bird!

5.

Bird...bird!
Yes, Little One,
But that's no ordinary bird
Dropped down five feet from you.
The black plume wagging on the head,
The white-lined mask on the face,
The blue breast
And brown-scaled belly,
Feet scratching for seed like a chicken,
All say quail.
He doesn't seem to belong here;
He looks like he flew out of China.
To be exotic isn't everything, though.
Look under this rock:
Six different beetles,
Each whirling in a circle
Scaled to its size.
Yet even the one whose circle
Is no bigger than the head of a nail
Holds in its tiny eyes
Precise replicas
Of the evening sun.

6.
Since you were born,
When I come home to an empty house,
It seems emptier than ever before,
Like a depot in a little town
That guessed wrong and never saw a train,
The people moved
To wherever there were more people,
The town went up for sale and never sold,
But when I come home
To papashouts
And tiny whirling dances,
The depot hums against the earth,
The trains roll madly by,
The house is a world,
The world is full.

7.

On our walks around the backyard,
You don't want to take my hand;
You want to find your own way.

I try to grab your hand
Because I want less trouble for me,
And you push it away

Because you want to touch everything:
The loose layers of ash bark,
The tongues of tigerlilies,

The leathery tabs of the jade plant
(If one comes off in your fingers,
It's the price of your science),

Soft grape leaves, the green
Scum at the bottom of the birdbath,
Even thorny branches of the bougainvillea.

I hope you stay like this.
I hope you always find
Your road only in the finding of it.

Don't let anyone lead you,
Even if they tell you again and again
You are lost.

8.

Estero Bay.
In this early light
The receding fog bank is pink at its edge.
In the pack on my back,
You find so much to look at
Your head bobs steadily
From sky to sand to sea.
Last night's tall surf beached
Hundreds of by-the-wind-sailors.
Their disc bodies and upright sails
Look like crumpled cellophane.
The few who were the mouths of the colony
Have midnight blue tentacles drying in the sun.
Scattered among them are brain-like
Blobs of sea pork,
Ropes of kelp on their floats,
And ticking waves of sand fleas.

Layers of red snappers must be moving in;
A brown cloud of pelicans
Stretches all the way to the fog.
Each time one dives, a gull drops beside it
To try to raid its pouch.
You murmur in my ear
When you spot an otter
Riding the swells on its back,
And your knees hammer my spine
When three harbor seals
Surface, bark, and then are silhouetted
Inside a lifting wave.

Right here yesterday
You suffered the biggest hurt
Of your little life.
You laughed and followed two children

Older than you.
As you looked up into their faces,
They pretended not even to see you,
Walked into you,
Knocked you down onto the wet sand,
And strolled away.
If you'd cried it would have been easier for us,
But you ran to your mother stunned,
Your eyes blank,
Your mouth a panting oval.
I wanted the sun to move so close
It would scorch human meanness from the earth.
There was no way to explain,
Even if you could have understood
All the words in the world.
All we could do was hold you,
And later take you to a huge rock
And point to the murre
Standing upright as a penguin.
As he preened,
A little light came back into your eyes.

By-the-wind-sailor, seal,
Pelican, murre.
Sometimes people will give you nothing
Or, worse than nothing, pain,
But the world is always
Something to see.

9.

There you are,
Asleep as you enter your second year,
And here I am,
Nearing the end of thirty-nine of mine
And counting:
This little scar keeps me awake tonight,
This little scar won't heal,
This little scar finds a home in the wind,
This little scar has none,
And this little scar
Says *I'm just me* all the way down.

After days of dead air,
I can't explain where a wind comes from
At this late hour,
But the poplar sways across the moon,
The maple bows to an old power;
I don't bend.
Prune a branch here,
Raise a crown of leaves there,
And suddenly the body seems to take on
A final shape.
Is that what frightens me tonight?
You change each hour,
Even in the flow of your dreams,
While I become a firm idea,
Flesh-rings hardening,
Will growing beyond anyone's reach,
Mind dense as an oak knot.

But come morning, your shriek of joy
Will make the wind of my heavy dreaming
Die down slowly,
Your arms will hold my head
Until my limbs go slack.
Could be I will change.
Could be you won't even care
If I'm changeless,
Unchangeable.

10.

You've never wanted to look down,
So your life is light as a midge's wing.

There *is* something down there,
And its face — too blank to read —

Is not our face,
And its song is the heavy clack

Of bone against bone in the mire.
We'll sit out that dance.

I'm learning from you:
The husk of my body is splitting,

My bones lighten to seed plumes.
Let's raise our arms, drift,

Catch an updraft,
And laugh in the face of gravity.

11.

It's nothing to mourn for.
I enter a room.
Under the low lights
Stands a 5'x 10' table with new felt
And hand-carved legs.
Paul Huebler is waiting,
And he hands me the finest cue he's ever made —
Black linen wrap,
Inlays of peroba, bubinga, and pau ferro.
It's a wand in my grasp, and I smile,
And he introduces me to the archangels:
Onofrio Lauri, Ralph Greenleaf,
Alfredo DeOro, Irving Crane,
Luther Lassiter, and Willie Mosconi.
Someone pokes his head in the door
To ask for a game of 8-Ball,
But he is banished by a stony silence.
We are serious men,
And 14.1 Continuous is our game.
One by one I play them.
I never scratch,
I never get cornerhooked,
I try a seven ball combination shot,
And the Lord says yes.
Of course, I lose to Mosconi,
But who cares?
It's a pleasure to play The Man,
And I have an eternity;
One of these eras I'll take him.
We all pause for a beer at the bar —
All except Lassiter, whose stomach is bad —
And I tell them about my wife and daughter,
And they say, "Ah, Hanzlicek,
You lucky bastard,"
And then it's back to the table.

12.
You're asleep.
Your mother is asleep.
Lifting over the ridge behind me,
The full moon
Casts a line of light on the water
All the way to the horizon.
On shore, a bonfire
Sends up spirals of sparks.
Sometime near midnight,
Grunion will ride the light
Onto the sand.
The drunks at the bonfire
Will rise and shout when cold water
Catches their ankles.
Flashlight beams will frame circles
Of wriggling, silver-sided
Helplessness.
Grunion aren't hooked,
They're not even netted,
They're just grabbed by cold hands
And thrown in a bucket.
I won't wait for midnight;
I'll join you and your mother in sleep.
I haven't a prayer now,
But I'll make some wishes:
May you never be helpless;
If you need help,
May you know where to find me;
May you always trust my hands,
And may my hands never hang at my sides
Too weak to help.
Goodnight,
And a little luck to the grunion.

3

Summer Night

Under the railroad trestle,
A few smog-bitten eucalyptus trees
Let go leaves
Into the windlessness.
The stars, obscured by haze
And the shimmer of rising heat,
Make navigation difficult,
So the derelict,
Kicked out of the mission
For bad behavior,
Enters his cardboard home
On hands and knees.
His life is simple:
He has no fire to tend,
Since there's no one to cook for
But himself,
And he's on a liquid diet.
He's a pilgrim,
In his sleep as wedded
To the earth as a worm,
And while he's awake,
Sustained by his blind faith
That there's no cure
Left in the world.

Bill's Well

We picked feed corn, hog's delight,
By hand,
Peeled back the shucks
And broke them off at the base of the cobs,
Tossed ear after ear
Over the high rails of the wagon.
Not a cloud,
Just numbed palms and fingers by noon
When we collapsed in the field
For green tea and bologna sandwiches.
Redwings followed us
All through the afternoon.
At sundown we went to the well.
The water bubbled up
On the backs of our hands.
Then we took off our straw hats
And pushed our heads into the cold flow.
And then we drank.
It made our eyes throb in their sockets
And left behind the tang of iron.
There were always a few grains of sand
At the bottom of the tin cup.
We drank long into the dark.

Fresno July

1. Morning

The grackle, greased by light,
Sounds his liquid bell,
And the dew vanishes.

The alarm has carried to the hive;
Bees report for work
In the factories of magnolia blooms.

By nine it's 90
And rising by the minute,
And the marigolds

Begin to sag in their beds,
Just as the mind begins
To sag and search for shade.

2. Noon

A driver on Blackstone Avenue
Accelerates
With a murderous touch of the foot.
He changes lanes and cuts me off,
But if I so much as look at him,
He'll hunt me down
To the last stoplight on earth.
I bend over the steering wheel
And delicately,
With forefinger and thumb,
Lift the soaked shirt from my back.
If the tatoo parlor
Wasn't closed for lunch,
I'd have an icecube
Burned into the nape of my neck.

3. Night

An hour ago,
I thought I heard the windchime
Clink once.
Now I'm not so sure.
The river is nine miles away.
I'm afraid if I laid down
Near its ribbon of stars
It would halt its flow,
Maybe even raise a cross-current wave
To block whatever breeze might be.
Not trust a river?
The old-timers
Say salmon used to spawn there.
They didn't arrive slippery,
But even worn to the coarseness
Of granite sand,
They made their horrible journey.
How does an instinct like that
Simply disappear?
It goes when trust goes.
Someone builds a dam,
And word runs up the river.
What is a dam?
It holds back water,
And it holds trust locked
In the cells,
It keeps
A tired man locked in his city.

Letters

In another country,
There's a man
Who has slept in my house,
Shared my food and wine.
He gets each of my letters,
But before he sits down to open one,
It's been read and resealed
By someone neither of us knows,
And that alters every move of my pen.
I choose words bare of meaning,
Not those that take wing.
Each paragraph is a closed white fist
With a tiny insect
Whirring at its center.
The whole letter must go into hiding
Like an animal
With only one cave in sight,
And that one
Filled with the scent of the human.

On a Highway South of Minneapolis

Three chestnut horses,
Wearing white
Saddles, stand on the beach
Of a wide sea of snow.
The elm trunks are black

On the lee sides,
White where they are driven by wind.
Each gust is a fight at the wheel
To hold the car
From taking wing like an osprey.

Red barns toss on the drifted waves.
Kitchen lights blinking,
White houses edge the vanishing point
Like liners in fog.
The word silo has a charged meaning.

The new ones cradle
What can cross oceans to kill.
I want to pull over,
Wade the wind across a field,
Open the door of an old-style silo,

And breathe
The heavy urinous smell of silage
Until I faint.
Or laugh out loud
In the joy of a pure memory.

One Humble Citizen

In the President's mind
Little swords
Are rattling darkly,
Like quarters in grandfather's
Deep right pocket.
They won't be beaten into plowshares,
They won't buy a child
Good 'n' Plenties for the Saturday matinee,
They'll put the bones of the poor
On a bus out of the city
For summer camp
At Lake Sleep-Forever.

Was my vote tallied?
After all, I'd established
Permanent residency on the avenue
Of scent between a woman's breasts.
I won't move from this house
As long as it has peace cornered,
But what's one humble citizen to do?
Stay in bed all day?
Stop retrieving
The morning paper from the rosebed?
Lock compassion in a trunk in the attic
Next to grandfather's shoes?

4

Insomnia

A mockingbird
Sang to his lady all night.
Now, just before sunrise,
A dog barks on the next street.
Inside me, it's very much the same:
I sang to my lady all night,
And a dog is telling me
To get up and make something
Of my life.
Work is good for you,
He says, it is ennobling,
Who does not work shall not eat.
To hell with it.
While the light tries the shutter,
One more song,
Maybe two.

Landlocked

For twenty-four years I was
Landlocked, and since my woman
Is very much like the sea —
Some days brooding like a fogbank,
Other days a mirror,
Always a mystery in the dark,
Learning so much
Of the world by touch,
Often quiet, yet hiding
The slow power
To reshape the rockiest coast —
It's good I didn't meet her
Until I'd seen the ocean
Under both sun and moon
And could understand.
Some.

Evening Rain

The edges of the clouds
Are blue as the burst veins
On the backs of my grandfather's hands.

He labored through some hard rains,
In the old country and this one,
To be twice my present age.

My pain has been a drop on a leaf
Next to what flowed through his life,
Yet I feel twice my age.

Then I turn to face you;
In an instant, I'm half my age,
Starting to be a man.

I step off the porch
To bathe my hands
In the stream from the downspout,

And then offer them to you,
Slightly wrinkled,
But unblemished by my time.

Body and Soul

There is the whisper
Of one shoulder against the sheet
As you turn in the dark.
Below that whisper,
I know there is a body:
Red chambers of the heart,
White bellows
Of the lungs working steadily,
Pink viscera,
Kidneys, liver,
And the maroon of the spleen.
When I said I loved you
Body and soul,
I meant the whole body.
Forgive the details.

Dear Ophelia

How sad
You are lost here with me;
I can't even
Decide my shoe size.
I look at a bone
To say something bright.

I look at myself,
And the world is a blur.
Don't go to the river.
Don't even think of the river.
The carp in its deeps
Only want to stir up
A cloud of silt,
A cloud of trouble.
We're classical lovers;
We ought to be clear.
Let the river flow black
And lonely in itself.
I wear size 10½.

The carp are nothing.
All I have to do
Is say I love you.
Is that all I have to do?

Don't even look at the river.
The sky is longer.
Believe me,
I'm a perfect 10½B.

Journey

My ticket is taken.
In minutes, mountains
Are little whitecaps
On a lake of red land.

Rivers fan out
Like scratched ink
Feathering on wet paper.
The gray roads are lost.

When the last landmark
Vanishes, I bail out,
Drift down to you,
Beginning and end of this

Long journey, this venture
Through the dry air
Around a single lamp
That burns through night.

Simple Truths

From 14,000 feet
The Q'eros look down on the clouds
And the rivers
Carved by a green snake
The creator dragged through the valleys.
Wood, corn, potatoes
Must be trudged up steep switchbacks;
The people are there
Because there the herds thrive.
The thin air floats the soft notes
Of a wooden flute,
And woven into them
Is the song sung to the herds:
Because you drink
We drink,
Because you eat
We eat,
Because you are
We are.

They also cling to the peaks
Because they know life
Gets less simple as it descends.
In Cuzco, men like them
Are beasts of burden
Driven early into the ground
By the loads they bear.
Better sharp stones on a mountain trail
Than cobbles laid down by slaves;
Better the burden
Of food for your children on your back
Than someone else's bale of rags.

Simple truths,
But Nezhdanov took his own life
Because he could not simplify himself.

More and more,
Things don't bother me,
Since they are as temporary as I am.

That's all I can tell you,
Dianne,
When you come to me at night
Weighed down by a day that grew too long.
Or I can take you outside
And point to the stars
And speak of our distance from them.

Or I can point to one other simple truth:
The light at noon
Hides the stars,
But the stars are there,
Just as when you feel you are alone
I am hidden
But there.
Because you drink
I drink,
Because you eat
I eat,
Because you are
I am.

5

The Long Arc

In my fortieth summer
I seem to look
Back as much as forward,
Trying to pick up little scraps
Of the past
Before they are carried away
On the sole of a shoe.

*

Getting ready for winter
In August.
Coal pounding down the tin chute
And rumbling into the bin
As my father and I shovelled.
By the end of the load,
We were black with white
Sweat streams down to our waists.
We showered under a 5 gallon pail
With a ring of holes
Drilled into the bottom
Hung from the cellar ceiling.

*

All down the street,
The smoldering fires of damp maple leaves
In the last light of evening...
The trick was not to run to a fire,
But to approach at a trot,
Like a ship nosing toward a pier,
And then to lift slowly
Into the long arc,
Inhaling deeply all through it.
We were three or four years
Out of a world war.
The ripeness of that smoke was held
In our hair for days.
All the deaths were still close.
People worried about each other.
Smoke was the first smell of morning.

*

I didn't know
He was standing in my shadow.
There was the crack
Of the ball on the bat
And then a duller,
Sickening sound.
He held his head in both hands
And ran hard up the hill.
His mother took him away
In a taxi and gave me
A look as I sat on the curb.
When he came home,
I watched his bedroom
Window each morning for two weeks.
Finally his mother
Raised the shade,
And a few minutes later
He drew back the white curtain
And waved.

*

The power plant steam whistle
Blew at five,
And men all over town
Put down their work for the day.
Lucky and I sat by the hedge.
We waited.
I stroked Lucky's long ears.
We waited several long minutes,
And then we saw
My father climbing the hill,
And we ran down to meet him,
Lucky pawing his denims,
Me looking up as he smiled
And his calloused hand came down
To cover the top of my head.
We could have played
A good while after the whistle,
But he was worth
Sitting down and waiting for.

*

I loved finding myself
Alone in the woods.
The stag beetle
Was my grotesque, armored friend
Who walked with a stutter.
There was a heap of sawdust
Where a piliated woodpecker
Had hammered his home.
The light always drifted down
In pieces: a little here, a little there
On the undergrowth.
Goldfinches were pieces
Of lateral light
Darting across the canopy.
On hands and knees
I looked down the dark tunnels
Of cottontail trails through the brush.
I was totally at one with nature
Until the day a passing bird,
One I couldn't even identify,
Shit in my hair.

*

The faint smell
Of raw dough and shortening...
Four flesh-colored mounds,
Molded by my mother's precise hands,
Rose in the pans
Under towels sewn from flour sacks.
The oven
Turned flesh to gold.
In that aromatic kitchen,
Who could wait
For the loaves to cool?
Butter melted on the steaming slabs.

*

Orest was a DP,
A ripple on a wave after the war.
Lithuania...Rumania...I forget...
Some miserable place where the postage stamps
On letters from his relatives
Were engraved with trams and tractors,
Dumptrucks and freighters.
He lived under low skies
In a gray house with gray trim.
He was fair game for anyone;
At recess, even the fat kids teased him.
But he soon quit crying
And began to learn
Something from each fight,
Grew steadily craftier and meaner.
One day the sun came out.
It was his turn
To taunt with his broken tongue:
Taig dat, you sunbitch.

*

It was slow going.
The skin of ice shattered
With each step
And my boots sank into a foot of snow.
Suddenly, out of the collapsed
Umbrella of an old pine,
Seventeen — I counted —
Ring-necked pheasant roosters
Beat their wings hard a few times
And then floated downhill
Into brown stalks of milkweed.
It's the sound that lingers,
The clacking panic,
And then the silence of the glide.
I had no gun.
I don't know where the hens were.
I never had the urge to shoot.

*

Uncle Bill and Uncle Louis
Honed their thin knives,
Then barred
The door to the shed.
Good thing, too.
When the deep piglet
Squeals started,
The yard-wide sow took a long run,
Slobbering with rage,
And rammed the door with her head
So hard the whole shed quaked.
Then out of the window
Came the testicles,
Tiny comets with tails of blood.

*

There were cold islands
All across the surface where springs
Boiled up from the bottom.
A girl and I left the gravel pit
And entered the woods.
In a clearing,
In full afternoon sun,
She lowered
The top of her bathing suit to her waist.
Her breasts were so new
They hardly moved when she moved.
It was all so new
I turned to stone, could only look.
She talked me into it.
She was a year or two older.
Maybe she was younger.
Maybe I talked her into it.

*

The storm drain
Was taller than I was.
For about a hundred feet,
I could look back
And see the O of light
Where I'd entered.
Then it took a right turn,
And it was always a contest
To see how far I would go
Into the dark,
Feeling my way
On the damp walls.
I was never much good at it.
I imagined rats
And worse: nothing but me
In the darkness forever.
Coming back around the corner
And running toward the light
Was like being born again,
Like saying no to guilt,
To the god I'd been taught.

*

When I wanted to think about nothing,
I walked to the river.
I sat down right where a lip of water
Curled over an eight foot dam.
Watching the surface
Sliding, sliding...I knew
I had time.
So much gone,
Yet there would always be more,
Coming around that bend
Where the willow dragged the ripples.
It seemed
There would always be more.

*

What do they add up to?
Snapshots...
A few memories of a boy...
Part of the shape of a man.
In the middle of my life,
I look back to that smaller self
And know that no matter what,
I'd rather be here, now.
Yet the little one stands inside me,
Often wants
To touch something — like this paper —
With my hand.